THE FUNNY THING ABOUT DEATH

CHANGING OUR "NO TEARS, PLEASE" CULTURE

DONNA LYNNE ERICKSON

◆ FriesenPress

Suite 300 - 990 Fort St
Victoria, BC, V8V 3K2
Canada

www.friesenpress.com

ISBN
978-1-5255-3449-2 (Hardcover)
978-1-5255-3450-8 (Paperback)
978-1-5255-3451-5 (eBook)

1. SOCIAL SCIENCE, DEATH & DYING

Distributed to the trade by The Ingram Book Company

DEDICATION

To the love of my life, without whom
my dreams would be buried with me.
Thank you, Rick Walker,
for enhancing my life and legacy.

TABLE OF CONTENTS

ACKNOWLEDGMENTS

My co-facilitator, Colette Howery, who taught me to lean into the discomfort of grief as we bear witness to the sorrow of loss.

My favourite Palliative Care Consultant, Pam Cummer, RN, who teaches physicians, patients and families how to take gentle care at the end of life.

My mentor, Dr. Alan Wolfelt, who continues to educate the world about his philosophy of companioning and walking alongside others in grief.

To the Camrose Primary Care Network and The Hospice Society of Camrose for supporting and encouraging community members who are working through loss.

To every single person in attendance at the bereavement and grief seminars we facilitate. Every story matters and through the telling of your story, we all learn.

The expert is within you—being written on your breaking heart.

May we all learn, together

THE FUNNY THING ABOUT DEATH

Americans think death is optional.

—Jane Walmsley

The funny thing about death is that we think we can avoid it—at the very least, control it.

The intention of this book is to explore our tendency, as a Western society, to dismiss grief as something to get over and move away from rather than face and work through. We all suffer loss, eventually, yet continue to try and buy our way out. We suffer loss and the aftermath of loss: raw emotions, untreatable pain and ongoing suffering of the bereaved. Often our response is to ignore, dismiss and avoid people who are grieving because they make us uncomfortable.

Many professionals, from hospital staff to morticians to life insurance providers, know death is inevitable—they see it happening every day.

The message of our privileged North American culture is that we need not suffer in any way. This enables us to live in denial saying we need not suffer in any way, shape or form. The marketers and merchandisers whitewash the reality of pain, aging and death by telling us we can buy products and services to prevent loss.

We do everything humanly possible to protect ourselves, prolong our life and avoid pain. We lock our doors, install security systems and mortgage big houses. We take vitamins, go on diets, and buy gym memberships. We use the right shampoos, skin care regimen and good drugs.

Most of all, we worry—like worrying can add a day to our life and prevent a hair from falling out of our head. We worry about keeping a marriage together, securing a lifelong career, preventing a drunk driver from swerving into our lane—or the path of a child or a friend or a parent.

On the other hand, literally, we receive news of great tragedy and destruction. The media interrupts our idealistic lifestyle with breaking news coverage. It used to be daily newspaper headlines on our doorstep every morning. The once-nightly news hour has taken over our living rooms all day long; add to that the constant barrage of loss on tiny screens 24/7 through our hand-held devices. There are vivid images of school shootings, catastrophic natural events and racial violence to name a few that continue to interrupt our comfortable lives and pierce the façade of bliss.

So what is it? Can we guarantee the loss-free lifestyle yet insert the reality of tragic events, and expect clarity? How do we process the conflicting messaging?

My Dad, the undertaker (not the wrestler), taught me covertly about death and dying. He did not realize what I was absorbing. Neither did I. He was often called away from home to 'pick up a body.' It was during the most poignant times that I learned. I put myself in the place of a classmate whose father died on Christmas Eve, in an armchair. The friend whose father had a heart attack and crashed into the ditch. A baby who was taken mysteriously, in her crib.

I overheard adult conversations. I remember Mom and Dad hugging each other as he told a story about a father who carried his lifeless daughter, wrapped in her quilt, into the funeral home. "She was wearing the same flannel pyjamas as Donna Lynne's."

I stopped wearing them, because in my four-year-old head, I was wearing her pyjamas. Then, I began to look suspiciously at my favourite quilt. Children gather information and process words and actions, literally, through imaginative minds. Death is no exception.

Up until that point in time, I thought death was only for old people. My grandparents were not even old enough to die. As I entered my teens, I couldn't imagine my grandparents dying. I panicked—how would I ever make it through that? Then they died. I survived; I cried; I miss them, still.

I grew up in a household where death was commonplace and traumatic at the same time. We believed that death was not the end of us, but there was a light at the end of the tunnel. God. Heaven. Eternal Life. All those promises weaving in and out of my life. I would be okay.

My Dad died in a hearse when I was 35 years old. I was not okay. That was the ultimate and most difficult lesson about death. He was only 60. I recently surpassed that milestone and breathed a sigh of relief. I often thought if my invincible Dad died so young, what was to stop Death from knocking on my door?

The gift from my father? Even in his death, which took some time to reconcile, I accept death is a natural part of life. Yet, with each loss, I have had to revisit that reconciliation work and with every passing year I understand the importance of mourning. I am learning that life is a never ending story of love and loss, despair and hope.

Not everyone agrees with me. There is a societal wide philosophy that refuses to acknowledge the fullness of death. The whole package includes accepting the life-changing power of grief and more importantly, the human heart's need to mourn.

Open discussion of death and dying was acceptable dinner conversation at my family table, but I have discovered in my relationships that not everyone feels this way. Death is a taboo subject. We can all talk about the beginning of life, but the ending is so mysterious, many people are fearfully superstitious.

With this introduction to The Funny Thing about Death, I hope you will contemplate your losses, come to understand your personal philosophy of bereavement, grief and mourning, and then be able to make a difference for our 'no tears, please' society mourners.

All the money in the world will not buy assurance. Guarantees are only lifetime, after all.

Author's Note: Throughout this book there is room to journal and doodle. Some of us use words, others may find doodling during contemplation more effective. Please make this practice your personal journey.

Loss creates ripples that disrupt serenity, security and schedules. It is either spontaneous or dreadfully expected. And we are never ready for it.

—D. L. Erickson

Make a list of people you knew who have died:

Choose one name from your list and describe your relationship to that person:

How did this person die?

THE EVENT

An odd by-product of my loss is that I'm aware of being an embarrassment to everyone I meet. At work, at the club, in the street, I see people, as they approach me, trying to make up their minds whether they'll 'say something about it' or not. I hate it if they do, and if they don't . . . Perhaps the bereaved ought to be isolated in special settlements like lepers.

—C. S. Lewis

The funny thing about bereavement is the way the bereaved are judged. Society decides if one qualifies to be considered bereaved and then the expectation is that one must follow a timeline. This timeline varies from one household to another, but the fact is, great expectations are placed on the bereft.

To be bereaved means something precious to me has been ripped from my hands, my heart, my personhood. Bereavement is a loss event.

What constitutes loss to such an extent that one is left with a bleeding severed limb, shocked, empty, stunned? Death does that, for certain. But what about divorce? Death is a final loss, so the divorced may not be validated, as say a widow's loss.

Do we consider the loss of health, mobility or mental ability as a bereavement event? Other less tangible losses: moving from the farm to town, leaving a job, broken friendship, a pet, a driver's license or a business. The ongoing loss of a loved one with dementia or Alzheimer's. The ongoing loss of living children when a family is torn apart and parents and children no longer speak. Grandchildren lose contact and it wasn't their choice.

We love comparisons. We thrive on competition. I hurt more than you.

"My loss is bigger."

Or worse yet, "My loss is not as bad as my neighbour who lost her granddaughter; after all, my mom was 85. I should be happy we had her for so long."

We invalidate our losses by comparing them to others. This not only shuts down our permission to mourn, but it puts into power a pecking order that judges loss, creating a master template upon which we base our philosophy of grief.

No matter what type of loss we experience, we need to go back to the reality of a bereavement event. When I experienced the loss of family members, dear friends, marriage broken by divorce, bankruptcy or career position I was bereaved each time. Something I held dear—a person, place or thing; had been taken unwillingly from me. It was taken and I had no control, super power or capability to hold on to it. I was left bleeding. My trauma betrayed me. Something happened in my heart, mind, body and soul.

My heart was rendered into two. There was immense pain and sorrow.

In fact, the shock of bereavement is so intense, our minds may need to slow down to protect our hearts. Our digestion slows down; our heart rate changes. We can be dazed and confused. Our soul cries out and there is no answer. There is no stopping, reasoning or bargaining power to delete the event.

We are designed to respond to trauma—fight, flight or freeze. Each loss is different and we are unique in our experiences. Our loss is best realized in small doses. If I am given a bottle of antibiotics for an infection, I can't short circuit the treatment by taking the whole bottle at once. I can't possibly take on the whole reality of my loss by having it all mentally sorted out in one moment in time.

We are lost for meaning and purpose, so we search, yearn and scream for answers. Why?

A roller coaster of emotions may present itself. Or we shut down those inner feelings to survive the immediate acute moments of loss.

Whether our loss is sudden, anticipated or ongoing, our life is changed forever.

If I lose a leg, I don't sprout another leg. If I pound a nail into my coffee table, I can pull it out, but the hole is still there.

Yes, my father died in a hearse. The irony would not be lost on him and because of his sense of humour, I know he would love to tell the story. This is one of my bereavement events. This is his story.

It was a hot July day in a very small town, Ashern, Manitoba. Dad and his boss had 'picked up a body' at the local hospital and were within a block of the funeral home. Suddenly Dad said, "Glen, I think you better drive. I feel funny."

My Dad was dead by the time Glen had opened the driver's side door. His large body, slumped over the steering wheel, was pulled to the pavement and Glen began CPR. They had been friends for life and now that life was in his hands.

A new RCMP constable was making her rounds and came across two men in black suits, struggling on the ground near the open door of a black van. She turned on the lights and pulled up. Imagine her shock when the one who seemed to be winning the wrestling match hollered and gestured to the unmarked black van, "Help me move the body in the back so we can put him in!"

The phone call came from Mom. She wasn't making sense. I phoned my children's father, with whom they were visiting for the summer. He would make some phone calls and find out what was happening.

In Saskatchewan, I had been enjoying an empty nest for the summer and barbecuing a steak on my little hibachi. Needless to say, that went uneaten.

The news of the death of my father changed me immediately—which happens when we human beings have been torn apart.

The old dictionary meaning for bereavement: To take away by destroying, impairing, or spoiling; take away by violence. I was bereft. My father, the most stabilizing force in my existence, was gone. I was alone, in a college town, quiet and empty for the summer break. There was one friend I knew I could call. Virginia was on my couch crying with me, immediately. She was my strength. She reminded me to sit down, to drink water, to breathe. She knew who to call for help.

I am grateful to the people who surrounded me that day. People who knew I couldn't be alone. Dwayne, my boss, drove six hours to pick up my oldest daughter, who was working at a summer camp. He knew I was not thinking clearly, my shock too new and the road trip would be too much. After a fitful night of sleep my daughter and I made the long trip home to Manitoba. Once there, an entire community embraced us.

What stands out most was the relaxed state of our family. Surrounded by his five granddaughters who taught us that children grieve organically—they cry, they play, they cry, they play. Their natural grief process was a reprieve to the constant presence of our loss. We were relaxed in the love for each other. We were all in shock and we gave each other space to sort through the days in our own way. Sleep was disturbed and my body was exhausted. Every morning was good for a nano second but then the slap of truth woke me up. While waiting for the funeral, it was a moment in time when we were dazed and confused, loved and abandoned, peaceful and horrified. What did this mean? Who was I now? Jalmar's daughter, still?

Each member of our family has their own interpretation of the experience—because we are unique in our grief.

Therefore, if we who are raised together are so different, is it no wonder the bereaved are judged by diverse community members?

May I just say, years later, preparing for my first stand-up comedy set, I remembered Dad's last words: "I feel funny." I should be so lucky.

— D. L. Erickson

List losses you have experienced apart from death:

Do you see these losses as bereavement events?

Tell the story of one of these losses:

Who validated your grief?

THE SADNESS

Stifle yourself, Edith!

— Archie Bunker

The funny thing about grief is that people try to stifle the sadness—both the bereaved and the observer may think it is best to keep it inside. In our 'no tears, please' society, we ask that you put a sock in it, smother it, plug it up and stuff it down. You see, we are a confused people who know somewhere in the back of our head that loss is inevitable, but not right now. Observing a grieving acquaintance says subconsciously, "Your grief reminds me that life is not pain free and I am uncomfortable with your sadness." Then, we consciously try to fix the pain, change the mood or step away because we feel awkward.

Instead of leaning into the discomfort of grief, we would sooner treat it. We keep busy to be distracted from reality, self-medicate to become numb, and cling to whatever advice—you can have another child, you're young enough to remarry or move onto new things— is an attempt to buy us comfort.

Well intentioned, but what we do to each other is deplorable .

I witnessed a pissing storm of clichés in a large church in Calgary, Alberta a number of years ago. My dearest friend was losing a sister to cancer when her other sister and her husband were suddenly killed. At the funeral luncheon, dozens of well-meaning people 'comforted' the family with comments such as these:

"They didn't suffer."

"They are with Jesus."

"God needed them home."

And of course, "They're in a better place now."

In the face of her heavy grief from losing her sister, those comments angered rather than comforted. She barely managed to maintain her composure and only did so to honour the children of the deceased. The lid blew off when we went outside for some fresh air.

"I just wish the fuck they would tell me how horrible this was and that they missed them terribly—and how about just saying they are sorry for our loss."

Can we please stop this?

I am a recovering born-again Christian, so I can say this: in some cases, our church culture has taken the flat edge of a drywall tool and smoothed over the holes of grief. I heard a preacher, from the pulpit, explain that he was not giving himself the permission to cry when his mother died because God was in charge and he would not question God's will. That poor man carried the burden of grief for a very long time. He did not allow the grief to exit into mourning. I question the effectiveness of his counsel of parish members if he was unwilling to reconcile his own loss.

In the name of God, according to etiquette of social function and by the shaming of voyeuristic judges, the bereaved, in their grief are stifled. There is no room for processing the bereavement event in a society that places expectations according to timelines and schedules and degrees of faith. Our cultural response to grief is so embedded into our fast-paced lifestyle. "It happened, my condolences, get over it, on with it and let's get back to normal!" Can we change? Will we change?

I remember when we smoked in every public place—the Greyhound bus, airplanes, hospitals, offices and libraries all had ashtrays! We have since changed our culture drastically. We started educating our children about the harmful effects of smoking. Students began scolding their parents at home. We were taught the harmful effects of smoking through advertising campaigns, by our health care providers and in the sharing of stories by those who were dying. These were some of the methods we used to create a new world. We all learned how to stand up for a much-needed safe environment.

It is time for a revolution to account for the effects of smouldering grief!

Since 2011, my colleague, Colette Howery, and I have held numerous workshops in Alberta, Canada. Our mandate, at the beginning, was to to help people understand "This thing called grief." We were to do only two workshops for the Alberta Hospice and Palliative Care Association (AHPCA) creating content around the theme for its annual Road Show. These AHPCA events were held in Camrose and Rimbey. A community member from The Village at Pigeon Lake asked if we would present a third workshop. We did and were amazed at the response—people gave up a day from their busy lives to come talk about grief!

Thanks to positive feedback, the physicians in Camrose involved in the local Primary Care Network (PCN) asked to have workshops hosted in the communities they serve. The framework we originally created for the day remains. It is the people, the experts in the room, who come sharing their grief who are the teachers. Therefore, every workshop is unique.

Such simple teachings have impacted our community at the same time other people have been leading the way in North America. It is time. There is a movement that needs momentum and if you are looking for one nugget in this book, please take this one thing: grief is not a disease. But if one does not have permission to mourn, the bereaved become diseased. We can create healthier communities by giving permission to mourn.

I digress. I will hop off my soapbox and get back to what I wanted to talk about in this chapter: it is the fact that grief is the internal sadness and sorrow that comes as a result of the bereavement event. We are human and like I said earlier, we are affected physically, mentally, emotionally, spiritually and socially, in our response to loss

What goes on in the body when loss occurs?

Physically our bodies react. We are holistic beings, so when our heart is breaking into two, our body sends the message to slow down. The digestive system slows down, the heart rate changes, stress hormones take a swirl and our breath gets shallow. We no longer enjoy the taste of food, or we eat too much searching for the pleasure we once had in food. We forget to tend to normal things such as drinking water, sitting down to rest or stretching our limbs. Virginia did this for me. She reminded me to sit, rest, drink water and breathe.

Emotionally, we are protesting, but our grown-up self may be cramming the screaming heart downward, into silent submission, felt only by the lump in our throat. Inside our swimming heads and breaking hearts we feel confusion, anger, fear, and a myriad of other emotions. How would my three daughters react to the news that their grandfather was gone? Dead. Their first experience of death. I suppressed my emotions thinking I had to be strong for them, for my Mom.

Mentally, we are scrambled. Barbara Fane writes in her article, "Grief Symptoms: How Grief Affects the Brain:"

Your brain is trying to recover. You are experiencing a deep biological response to your loss, just as you are experiencing physical, psychological, and emotional responses. Hormones and chemicals are released, internal reactions are disrupted, important bodily systems shift into emergency mode.

It was so important that people helped me sort through the process of travelling to Manitoba. I was ready to take off immediately, but they knew my mind was not clear to safely drive.

Spiritually, we feel abandoned. What we once deemed safe, secure and meaningful has changed. Numb to the thunk of reality, it is hard to process what has happened to our beliefs, religious or not. We are yearning and searching for meaning. Why? Why did my Dad die so young? It wasn't fair. As babies, we yearn, seek and cry when we are uncomfortable. When we are bereaved it is our natural tendency to yearn for comfort, seek meaning and cry in pain.

Socially, we may not realize the full effects until we are in the mourning process. At first, people gather to hold us up. There are some who will ignore our loss because of their own discomfort—not knowing what to say or do, so they disappear from our circle of friends. We are looked at differently when something devastating happens. There can be a very real feeling of isolation. Divorced at 27, I left a world of couple friends and became a fifth wheel. A dear friend who lost a child says her loss changed her address book. When we lose a career our circle of friends, those we spent every day with, shrinks.

When we are grieving, our perceptions change. Our hearts yearn for the time before the loss. My Mom was very distraught that we were all together at the funeral luncheon and Dad's body was back in the garage at the morgue waiting to be shipped off for cremation. Jalmar, missing a funeral lunch? He was not only the undertaker but served as the minister for many funerals. In fact, he had been stressed that the local ministerial association had it in for him. They complained that 'some mortician' was doing all the funerals in and around town. There happened to be new ministers at several churches that spring and that spawned the inquiry. Another 'funny thing about death' is the way that Dad viewed this stressful situation with his typical sense of humour: "I think they are concerned that I am body and soul snatching!"

Everyone was grieving. A small community that lowered the flag and closed the post office on the day of his funeral. The community hall was packed and overflowing—something that made me proud but did not impress my brother, "It is our father who died." And that shows the differences within family when we are grieving. Neither one of us was right. We grieve differently. No judgement. As we made our way to the viewing with our two aunts, our father's sisters, we were discussing the community reaction. One of Dad's sisters was as pleased as I was. The other said she was angry and totally understood my brother—two sets of squabbling siblings a generation apart.

Pay attention to children. They observe us. They hear and see things that they take literally—in ways that we may miss. One granddaughter, seeing Grampa in the casket, asked why they cut him in half.

Wisely, Glen understood things from her perspective. He lifted the bottom lid of the casket and showed her that Grampa was still very much intact.

The funeral is a time for family to be embraced by the community. We all grieve uniquely and there are many who prefer no public event. Often, they are 'should all over' and begrudgingly live up to the expectations of the culture. I for one, due to my extrovert personality, appreciated the occasion. Talking, telling stories and seeing other people who cared about my Dad were important to me.

A family acquaintance, Ruth, gave me the perfect gift. She said, "I was just talking to your Dad last week. He told me how proud he was of you." She could have been afraid to tell me that, in case I cried. She could have kept that thought to herself, but she had the wisdom to know talking about something my Dad said about me was worth the risk. I vividly remember her words. And, I had permission to cry.

The funeral was not about mourning. It was about ritual. It was the start of our 'grief going public' as Dr. Alan Wolfelt explains so throughly in his writings. His book, "Grief Day by Day" is a must read. We embraced the support and love from others in our community, in our family and with our dear friends. When Dad's funeral was over, I crashed. I did not realize the physical and emotional toll on my body. We were all done in. Exhausted.

The mourning had not yet begun. Another misunderstanding in our Western culture is that the funeral is 'closure.' There is no such thing as closure in my life. The person who died is not closed off. The mourning is our external expression of grief and this is the time we are most guilty of suppressing because we may be too ashamed of our feelings we don't invite social interaction.

My Dad is no longer present physically—he has now shifted to the presence of memory.

When you would rather turn away from someone who is suffering a loss, learn how to press into their discomfort. Let them teach you

—D. L. Erickson

Describe your feelings when you were grieving:

Who told you not to be sad?

Who tried to fix your pain?

Write an **imaginary*** letter to that person:

*Please do not send such a letter, as this is an exercise to help you work through your stifled mourning, not to change the behaviour as another person. Sometimes burning or shredding the letter is a tangible way to let go of the pain.

THE FUNNY THING ABOUT MOURNING

Lament: to feel or express sorrow or regret for: to lament his absence . . . a formal expression of sorrow or mourning, especially in verse or song; an elegy or dirge.

—Dictionary.com

The funny thing about mourning is the embarrassment we cause others!

Mourning is different than grieving because it is the outward expression of the inner sadness called grief. It is a public display of acknowledging our pain. It is letting the sorrow show through—our eyes, our voice, in our actions and by our rituals.

It wasn't that long ago, we knew who was 'in mourning'—if not for the fact that we were less transient and went to everyone's funeral, we also could tell by tangible symbols of death. A veiled woman, a man with a black arm band or a family with a wreath on the door—wearing our heart on our sleeve. It wasn't so we could be warded off—indeed, quite the opposite. It was an opportunity to listen—to invite the mourner to share her or his story of loss. It was commonplace to ask questions:

"What was his name?"

"How did he die?"

"How old was she?"

"Where did you meet?"

"What did she do?"

We don't seem to have time to do this anymore. We don't take time to ask the questions. Worse than that, we don't take time to listen. Perhaps we assume we know the answers or that it is none of our business. The breakdown of our 'connectiveness' is ironic now that we are connected in so many ways due to technology— the network spanning the world changes the way we relate. It has been said the eye is the window to the soul and maybe this has added to our lack of understanding. We don't see pain in and through another person's eyes. There is a prevailing misunderstanding about mourning. It is seen as weakness; we accept a measured amount of tears, but when our behaviour changes after our loss, observers are skeptical.

Mourning is a slowing down, a re-evaluation of our new normal after a loss. There is no 'recovery' from grief. However, there is a way to reconcile our reality. We can reincorporate joy and laughter and meaning. It takes work. Hard work. This work is not successfully done in isolation; it takes a companion.

Dr. Alan Wolfelt explains his philosophy of companioning in his book "Companioning the Bereaved: A Soulful Guide for Counselors and Caregivers." One question of self examination stood out to me.

"If your desire is to support a fellow human in grief, you must create a 'safe place' for people to embrace their feelings of profound loss. This safe place is a cleaned-out, compassionate heart. It is the open heart that allows you to be truly present to another person's intimate pain."

Without safe places, in the rush hours of today's Western culture, we find it difficult to be an honest mourner. It is dangerous to be real with our grief because judgement creates more pain. In order to reconcile a loss into our life, we must find a safe person who will bear witness to our story. If we are brave enough to reveal our innermost thoughts and then we are treated with disdain, shame or harsh treatment, it may seal our grief forever.

What does mourning look like? It is as unique as our fingerprint. I may need to journal and write. To talk about Dad and share his funny stories. I am prompted to pick up the phone and give him a call when I see someone from our past or hear the geese coming back in spring. My brother will have done things differently. Same family environment—fished from the same gene pool. That should explain, then, how much more we differ from our friends and neighbours but does not explain why we all expect the same mourning processes.

Our personality also influences the way we show our grief. Extroverts will behave differently than introverts. Logical types may process the loss from the intellectual viewpoint, while the intuitive person's behaviour stems from 'large feelings' experienced. Those who are task oriented will have a hands-on approach—the more tangible, practical methods of working through grief.

Whether we analyze the facts, dance the feelings, sing the story or build a monument, it is an expression of our grief and should be celebrated, not mocked.

Why are we so hesitant to accept that mourning is a natural process of life? Organically, children grieve. Watch them. They know how to incorporate play to take a break from the sadness. Still very tender and aware, they need to be told the truth. Do not assume children do not understand. They are literal.

My daughter, at three years of age, watched our household wait for a friend's body to surface after a drowning. It took several days. Adults use the term body, as one unit when describing the deceased.

After the second night she asked, "Why do they just have his head?"

It set me back, "What do you mean?"

"Why do they just have his head and not his body?"

The most heartbreaking stories I hear in our workshops are those that involve the ignorance of adults who think children should not be exposed to the dying, the dead, the tears or the illness.

"I loved my Gramma to bits. I was not allowed to go to her funeral. I was not told how she died or allowed to speak about her then and even now."

"My infant brother died when I was eight. I never got to see him or go to his funeral."

"She was gone. Poof! My mother was replaced by a neighbour who cleaned our house and babysat my siblings. When she married my father, all of my mother's belongings disappeared."

Children who attend funerals of an aunt or a sister or a mother and are allowed to ask questions are better able to reconcile their loss. When brought into the family fold, the sense of belonging creates a safe place for them to sort out their thoughts and ask questions without having to fill in the spaces by using their active imagination.

Children of divorce can reconcile the truth of the loss of a parent in the family home when parents can put down the battle axes. If children can ask questions and have honest answers then fears can be acknowledged, which gives them assurance that they are loved

If we punch down the reality of sorrow, we all lose.

Here is an excerpt from my personal journal that reminds me of the hard work of mourning that helped me to reconcile my losses. I lived 'without' for nine months—without income, without a lover, without a home, a car, Internet, cable tv or a cell phone.

It was during this time that I discovered and had freedom to keen. It started when the geese flew south. The honking reminded me of Dad, how he enjoyed the thrill of scouting fields for good hunting spots. A lump started in my throat. Instead of suppressing it, I thought, why not let it out. I am most certainly alone in a house. I wailed and sobbed until I could no longer. I mourned the losses over a span of nine months. Beginning from my earliest memories to the present day. Here is what came of that spontaneous eruption:

They came as droplets at first. The tears of sorrow. Oozing as I wrote in my journal. Giving myself permission to release them, one portal at a time, brought healing to my soul. Finally, I opened the floodgates and I cried and wailed and emptied myself until there was nothing left.

One loss at a time. And soon, each morning I looked forward to my keening practice. Allowing the pain, fear and sorrow to walk up my throat and barge through once-clenched teeth. I opened my mouth and released the sour gas of squelched emotions.

I knew while I journaled and meditated and prayed—whether in music or silence—I would be just a little more connected. It was not an easy journey. I was disconnected before I could reconnect. I unplugged from the busyness of my life—left a marriage that was killing me, a business that held my head under water and a list of obligations written by a desperate woman—me.

Love, presence, serenity and hope are the blossoms of my soul's rest.

—D. L. Erickson

Who was the first adult you saw crying and what were the circumstances?

What did your family teach you about mourning?

Are you willing to outwardly express your sadness?

THE SPIRAL

It has been said, 'time heals all wounds.' I do not agree. The wounds remain. In time, the mind, protecting its sanity, covers them with scar tissue and the pain lessens. But it is never gone.

—Rose Fitzgerald Kennedy

The funny thing about our 'no tears, please' culture is that we think if grief is ignored or buried we assume it has gone away.

Grief does not dissipate in the hourglass of time. Time does not heal all wounds; it is what is done within time that helps us to heal those wounds.

If we need surgery to repair a broken hip but opt to put on a Band-aid the hip does not heal. The shattered bones will rip nerves, tear flesh and fester to the point of demanding attention. That is quite an emotional word picture that some would think over-exaggerates my point. But, does it?

Please take a minute and consider our chronic diseases, addictions, relationship breakdowns and community meltdowns that could be traced back to the festering wounds of grief trauma.

Because natural grief is not a disease or a mental illness, medical treatment is not necessary in most cases. That is not to say one should stay away from physicians but it is to say that grief is natural. As natural as childbirth. Unless there are complications, of course.

There are moments of grief bursts when we catch a familiar scent, hear the melody of a favourite song, glimpse sight of a beautiful scene or for no reason at all. Tears come like the gentle rain or a tsunami; raging rivers can swell from rippling brooks. We cry for a long time, but not all the time.

I witnessed a grief burst about the age of 12. My mother suddenly stopped to stare into the alcove of a store window in Moose Jaw, Saskatchewan. I looked up to her and wondered why we were looking into the window of an insurance agency. We were shopping and having a pleasant time yet tears were pouring down her cheeks. She was ashamed at them and wiped them away quickly saying, "I don't know what is the matter with me."

I do now. Nothing. Nothing was wrong with her. She was grieving and had no place to mourn. Her youngest sister, living far away in California, was only 24 and died from complications due to heart surgery. A surgery Mom had assured her was a simple procedure and could have been done years previous. Her sister Vi was excited to discover they were going to have a baby, but the doctors warned her the hole in her heart must be fixed, before she gave birth. But, Vi and the baby she was carrying, died days after what appeared to be a successful surgery.

Money was scarce. All that Mom could do was send a reel-to-reel tape of a solo she sang, to be played at Vi's funeral. She never went and it was a regret, a resentment and a sour memory of the Bible college community where we were living.

Everyone needs a safe place to tell their story. She did not feel safe. She never reconciled her losses by working through them. She only felt the guilt of not being able to 'get over' them.

Decades later, within months of my father's death, my mother's layered losses began to add up. Her father died. She helped her sisters nurse him through to the end of life, her brother was tragically killed and what she wanted most was to move to California where her family all moved in the 1950s. She was the only one to stay behind.

Then she found herself in trouble with her addiction to prescription drugs. While in counselling, she was granted permission to mourn. "Mrs. Erickson, you have suffered some significant losses in a very short amount of time."

"I should be able to get over it!" Again, scolding herself. After all, she had 'gotten over' her mother's and sister's and husband's deaths, just fine. "Haven't I?"

When she was 12, her mother died. It was in the forties when tuberculosis was claiming lives both from death and distance as infected people were locked away from their families in sanitariums. Imagine, living the last months of your life waving from the third-floor window to your children across the river. Five little girls wondering why mommy had left them.

Her father soon remarried and she was an angry teen. There was no room to mourn, to lament her mother's illness and death. Her grief was internalized and festered into full-scale prescription drug addiction and alcoholism. A terrible thing for a missionary family's son to have married. (Insert a whole load of shame, here.)

When grief is disenfranchised or ignored or numbed, it doesn't disappear. It festers, it percolates and it does not lie down. Our bodies betray us; they talk about us in ways to which we eventually have to pay attention. Chronic disease, addiction, mental illness—it's all about breaking down. Then we need intervention far beyond the skills of friends and family.

I am convinced that grief is not only about death; it is about suffering a loss. What is precious to me may not be precious to you. We are all different and each circumstance of loss is different.

Loss through death is more easily understood. Society allows a limited amount of grace, so generally, we put up with a few tears from the bereft. Acceptable—for a time. How long do we put up with this discomfort? The uncomfortableness that comes from being the observer? Typically, it is a timeline that fits within a three- to five-day bereavement leave from a job. Then get back at it and don't you dare miss next month's deadline.

Perhaps we will overlook as many as three months for a widow to rid the clothes from his closet. Any longer and we deem her mentally bonkers with the click of our collective tongues. We permit time to get through a full year of 'firsts' if a child or parent has passed. After that, we grow impatient and either 'should' all over them or insulate ourselves by stepping away. We often can't bring ourselves to say the "d" words—dead, died, and deceased much less say the name of the person who is no longer present physically.

We give ourselves credit by thinking we have the power to make grieving people cry. Guess what—they are still crying whether we see it or not. How lonely it is to cry alone.

Grief is the sadness that occurs within. It can be so powerful that it really can break the heart. There is something called Takotsubo-cardiomyopathy (broken-heart syndrome). When we hear someone has died from a broken heart, that literally could be true.

Grief is a deep, gut-wrenching feeling of sorrow and is most often expressed by tears. Tears can signify mourning as it is one external expression of that emotion. There are other ways to mourn. Not all mourners cry. Some express their grief in anger, silence, meditation, doing something physical—building, destroying or creating.

It is confusing to a society that has unwritten rules about mourning. We make decrees and statements about the bereaved. Enter the judgement phase of loss—we see effects of sorrow and they make us uncomfortable.

Stiff upper lip, and all that.

"She was so strong at her daughter's funeral."

"He gave his brother's eulogy and didn't shed a tear."

"She is coming back today. No one mention her grandson's death. We don't want to make her cry."

A divorce is a huge loss, especially if one is not the instigator. We don't often give permission to a friend to grieve the loss of a spouse through divorce.

"He was no good anyway. You are better off without him!"

"She was always flirting. You should have seen that affair coming. We all did."

Loss of a pet may be something you can't understand.

"It was just a cat! For Pete's sake, she is acting like she lost a child!"

"A horse! Like you will miss a horse, oh brother! In some countries, they eat horses, don't they? A dog I can understand!"

The rush to get our aging relatives into a safe place, out of their home, off the farm, to our community so we can see them more often (life is so busy) or into a care facility does not give time to the person at the centre of the loss. Feelings of unexpressed grief are brushed under the rug because they will protest too much. "Oh, mother! It is hard on me, too! You will get used to living in the lodge."

Loss of a job through downsizing or retirement is going to have a profound impact on the daily life of that person. "It's just a job. Nobody died!" A piece of us dies when we suffer loss. It's not only the loss of income but the loss of position, meaning or purpose—the loss of future dreams.

All of these and so many more typical protests and downplaying of events devalue the pain of loss. Which stifles grief. Which prevents the cleansing power of mourning.

When we drive the grief of others with the hammer of our expectations, we are doing harm. If we think it is helpful to plug up the tears of a mourner or apply clichés to smooth the rocky surface of grief, we can create a cover so heavy, the person may never try to lift it again. It will lift, however—sometimes from the pressure cooker of festering pain or it may resurface at another bereavement event. Unacknowledged soul pain sits in wait until there is an outlet for release.

When the red flags show up, we need more than companioning. When physical health deteriorates because of lack of self-care—lack of proper rest, eating issues, use of mood-altering substances, poor hygiene or suicidal ideation, we need help to be of help. There may come a time where companionship must be turned over to professionals. If we are walking a grief journey with someone and see these warning signs, we need to get help. It is beyond our ability as a friend. Invite your friend to go with you to a doctor, counsellor or emergency room. Ask another person to help you make that happen, if need be.

One widower described the depth of his despair to the point of suicide. It was New Year's Eve and he had a loaded gun, across his knees, having one last drink. If it weren't for the intervention by way of a phone call from his granddaughter he would not be alive.

There have been several occurrences during our seminars where red flags are raised—most often with those who deem themselves experts and are going to fix an acutely grieving person. These self-declared saviours are dangerous.

One man said he was helping a widow by telling her to get over her sadness: "What would your husband say if he saw the state of you?" Shaming is like a shotgun to the soul.

Manipulation of any type is mean. This person does not have what it takes to be a grief helper—not every person can nor should be. Whether by a character defect of control and manipulation or by their nature— better some people remain stuffing envelopes or giving donations to an organization such as a hospice or hospital. Please don't work with people—much less delicate people—if you have not worked through your own grief. If you do not understand the process of natural grief and mourning or have an agenda apart from the well-being of others.

Another man came into our session proclaiming the promises of God in the scripture as the only answer. Basically, he was saying that this business of mourning was unnecessary. That we lacked faith if we couldn't just 'get over it.' While the promises of God are sometimes a great support to individuals, we all still need to do the work of mourning. This man expected to find a target to convert and thumped the leather-bound King James with his fist to drive home his point. He is an extremist. Even people with a healthy, faith-based viewpoint need to understand that we must never pull a person to the position of transcendence. No one else can do the work for another. If someone declares to be an instrument of the Almighty, and creates fear, guilt, shame and power, they are dangerously dangling the faithful from a precipitous—this person is harmful.

It is exhausting for a bereaved person to know what they need. It is unfair to take over their journey—well intentioned or not.

Dr. Wolfelt wrote "The Mourner's Bill of Rights." It is written in many of his books but it is also easy to find the document on his website at www.

thecenterforloss.com. Use these words for yourself if you are in mourning. Post it on a locked front door if you are being hammered by people who are causing more harm than good.

No one is an expert at grief, except the person experiencing the loss. No one has the power to fix, to heal or to make things normal again. What we as a society have the power to do, unfortunately, is to stop the mourning process. We may do this, unaware of how harmful we are acting. To shame someone for their unique mourning rituals is to push their grief back down inside and they may never have room for the process to work. Working through our loss is hard work. It hurts; we cry. It seems never-ending—too big to face. Of course it does!

—D. L. Erickson

Who hindered rather than helped you during a loss event and how could they have done better?

Who instills hope within your soul?

Write a thank-you card to someone who was a good grief helper, Perhaps, this one you will want to send:

THE SHIFT

Those snowflakes sure are small, but when they get together they sure are mighty powerful.

—Some guy in a blizzard, in a
truck, in a ditch (is my guess)

The funny thing about shifting our culture is how easy it is, once we start. Eldridge Cleaver said, "There is no more neutrality in the world. You either have to be part of the solution, or you're going to be part of the problem."

We want the problem fixed, yet we sit on our hands, keep our thoughts and feelings to ourselves, even when we know it isn't right. If you read this book to the end, you may well be part of the solution.

What's your first step? Examine your own beliefs about death, dying and all the bereavement events you see around you every day. Pay attention to people in grief. They will teach you if you listen to their story.

Think of things you have experienced and record your thoughts about each loss. What is your story? Tell it to someone in writing or vocally—with someone you trust who will validate, actively listen without interruption or apply a solution to fix your grief.

Journal and explore your own expertise. Ask your circle of influence how they have seen you walk through losses.

Ritual is a helpful way to work through the rivers of loss and mark our life events as important. The traumatic pivotal points in our life, whether good or bad, direct us toward today. I stopped at a raging river, tossed in a rock that symbolized a bad relationship so I could let go of my regrets for making choices that led to a marriage. I have burned items in a barbecue that tied me to a memory of abuse. There are some pieces of gold jewellery at the bottom of a stream— because tossing them into the water was a ritual that symbolized to me "Goodbye, painful memory.".

When I hear the geese honking hello in the spring and goodbye in the fall, my heart is warmed by remembering my father.

My mom used to say, "Isn't this nice?" during those times when everyone was together and having a good time.

Now, in her memory, one of the women in our family will repeat that phrase and we all say, "Ah, I wish Gramma Chris was here!"

I have written letters to my parents to say goodbye as they each died suddenly. I keep precious little mementos that once belonged to them. I keep them close as I write or read.

'Remembering well' is a topic with which we have the most fun at the grief seminars Colette and I facilitate. One thing many authentic mourners have in common is ritual. There are fascinating and creative ways to 'remember well.' Find out how other people remember well. It takes time to listen. The reward is invaluable.

Awareness, education, action and maintenance. I hope you have a new awareness of what is happening today—the sanitization of death, the denial of inevitable losses, the methods to suppress and control, and the attempts to erase the pain of loss.

Have you a new awareness by reading this book? Read other books, do Internet research and most effectively, ask people face-to-face, "What's your story?"

Working as a Health Care Aide was one of the most rewarding careers for me. Having the privilege of entering a person's room, which is their home, and seeing the photo of a deceased spouse, child or former home created opportunities to ask questions. How did you meet? How many children do you have? What kind of work did you enjoy?

Do not use trusted relationships as a motive to intrude, but to show compassion. Allow the story to be told so those who have moved from presence to memory can be remembered well. Always maintain confidences and respect the stories of others.

Educate yourself by reading more and asking more questions. Volunteer—there is always excellent training available when you find a good organization where you can donate your time. In her book, "Feeding My Mother: comfort and laughter in the kitchen as my mom lives with memory loss," Jann Arden says, "Taking care of people makes you a better person. Period."

Be pure in your intentions. Facilitate rather than preach. Shift perspectives by asking questions, by not having all the answers. Make a difference by kindness, in love and with joy.

Maintain good health by walking the infinite path of loss and hope. It is an ongoing process. Rest when you must but don't stay stuck. Stuff happens. Despair is real; hope is possible. We may need to set apart time to explore our losses and test the waters that are new to us. Have a spotter. Don't do it alone. Lifting the heavy load that life sometimes deals us can be crushing, so find a friend. Be a friend. Be a grief helper, not a grief hinderer.

A Grief Helper is a companion to those who are bereaved; understands how to integrate loss into his or her own life, first; allows the bereaved to mourn in their own unique way; provides a safe place where the bereaved can express their pain and tell their story without judgement; knows the red flags of complicated grief and where to refer for professional help.

—D. L. Erickson

What is your 'take away' after working through this information about Bereavement, Grief and Mourning?

Are you hopeful about reconciling your own losses?

What is the first baby step you will take to help change the culture of our 'no tears, please" society?

I invite you to share your ideas, feedback and creative changes, to the level to which you are comfortable at www.facingloss.com.

ABOUT THE AUTHOR

Having lived in all the prairie provinces, Donna Lynne Erickson celebrates small-town life experiences and enthusiastically embraces her Canadian heritage.

Working in healthcare since 1999 in Public Relations, as a Healthy Workplace Facilitator and most recently on the front lines as a Health Care Aide, she combines those experiences into cofacilitating unique bereavement and grief educational workshops.

She lives in Sherwood Park with the love of her life, Rick Walker. Between them they have ten lively, lovely grandchildren and are thankful for the five amazing women (and assortment of sons-in-law) who share their lives, love and company.

AUTHOR'S NOTE

Disclaimer: There are no experts in grief. Least of all, me. The words that you read in this book come from my own opinion, observations and education gleaned from my life-long learning 'portfolio' of experiences.

I began writing this little book to give a sample of my philosophy of bereavement, grief and mourning in order to inform organizations and businesses, churches and community groups that may want to host a grief workshop, forum or education day which I call: Facing Loss, Together. And then my personal story leaked onto the pages and a very different book is published.

I have not given up hope that we can change the way we treat those who are suffering acutely. To understand and learn how mourning our losses (no matter what type) is a natural progression of life; there is no shame in grief.

I hope you are provoked to consider learning how to provide safe space for someone to mourn, reconcile and heal.

For more information please contact me at: www.facingloss.com or donnalynne@me.com

Printed in Canada